SAN ANTONIO

Text by
John W. Gilbert

Photos by
Andrea Pistolesi

BONECHI

Text by John W. Gilbert

Photographs from the archives of Casa Editrice
Bonechi taken by ANDREA PISTOLESI.

Photographs on pages 62, 63: Fiesta Texas pho-
tographs by Michael Murphy.
Photographs on page 60, 61: Copyright © 1993
Sea World, Inc; *All rights reserved; Reproduced*
by permission.
Photographs on pages 7, 8, 9, 31 below, 34a (by
Al Rendon), 34b, 34c, 40 (by Al Rendon), 57 (by
Al Rendon), 58 (by Al Rendon), 59 (by Al
Rendon): Credit to San Antonio Convention &
Visitors Bureau.
Photograph on page 41b: Credit to John Dyer for
the Majestic Theatre.

Printed in Italy by
Centro Stampa Editoriale Bonechi.

ISBN 88-8029-099-1

TABLE OF CONTENTS

INTRODUCTION

Welcome to Texas! And bienvenidos a San Antonio — a multiethnic metropolis in the Southwest with a unique history and cultural background which have made it a mecca for pioneers, immigrants, and visitors in general for some 300 years! Humorist Will Rogers called it "one of America's four unique cities." Indeed, San Antonio has been unique from its very origins as **Yanaguana**: a thriving village of the indigenous Coahuiltecan Native Americans at the time of Columbus' inauspicious arrival in the Caribbean from Europe in 1492.

The village was "discovered" by Spanish explorers in 1691 on the feast day of St. Anthony of Padua, and they promptly renamed it **San Antonio de Bejar**. Soon San Antonio, a half-way point between the ill-fated missions in East Texas and the Presidio of Northern Mexico in Saltillo, was to have no less than five Spanish missions. Since then six different flags have flown over the city, representing in turn imperial Spain and France, the Republics of Mexico and Texas, the Slave States of the Confederacy, and ultimately the U.S.A.

After the suppression of the indigenous Native American cultures and languages during the 18th century, three principal languages came to be spoken in San Antonio: Spanish, English, and German. Today most city residents are bilingual, although the Hispanic community has always made up the majority of city residents. In fact the latest census shows Hispanics — chiefly **Hispanics** — currently representing over fifty percent of the city population.

This essentially Hispanic heritage has blended well with the cultures of dozens of other ethnic communities from around the world, resulting in a vibrant mix which makes San Antonio a truly different, amazing city, as is amply reflected in its numerous festivals, its varied cuisine, its myriad customs, and its eclectic architecture. Old adobe buildings and Spanish Colonial missions survive alongside modern skyscrapers constructed in many different architectural styles. It is true that there is manifest economic disparity, with poverty existing alongside great wealth, but the city nonetheless possesses a festive multicultural "**ambiente**" attracting over 10 million visitors annually. It is no wonder San Antonio, a real "melting-pot," was named "All-American City" in 1949, '51, and '82.

CULTURAL ATTRACTIONS

Among the city's many cultural attractions are fine museums, the **San Antonio Symphony**, various performing arts groups, the **San Antonio Ballet**, and numerous other dance and theater companies, as well as touring Broadway shows. In addition, the city hosts a sizeable colony of artists and artisans from all over the world, and there are many fine galleries. Sports include professional NBA basketball with the **San Antonio Spurs**, minor league baseball with the **San Antonio Missions** (a team formed back in 1888), grand prix racing, year-round tennis, and nearly twenty year-round golf courses. There are also dozens of public pools and over a hundred city parks.

UNIVERSITIES

San Antonio is an important center for higher education as well, with over a dozen colleges and universities, and a large student population. The **University of Texas at San Antonio** was established in 1973, and boasts a 600-acre campus. **St. Mary's University**, founded in 1852, is the city's oldest. The prestigious **National Autonomous University of Mexico**, one of the oldest higher education institutions in the Americas, has its only branch outside of Mexico in the city. And since the 1980s, San Antonio has become an increasingly important center for hi-tech industries, as well as biotechnology and medical research. The **South Texas Medical Center** in northwest San Antonio has undergone particular expansion and growth.

LOCATION

Today San Antonio is the ninth largest city in the U.S., and the third biggest in Texas, with about a million inhabitants. A Sunbelt city in south central Texas situated at the edge of the Texas Hill Country and the Gulf Coastal Plains, it is the seat of **Bexar County** (pronounced "bear"). The climate is warm and sunny, with an average annual temperature of 68.8° F, and some 300 days a year of clear, blue skies. Corpus Christi and the Gulf Coast beaches are 140 miles away — about a three hour drive southeast — but there are also seven lakes within an hour's drive. Laredo and the Mexican border are 150 miles south of San Antonio, while the state capital of Austin is 80 miles to the northeast. Mexico City is 900 miles due south.

TRANSPORT

San Antonio is well-situated on major highways, the national rail system, and bus lines, and is served by the **San Antonio International Airport**. Getting around the downtown area is no problem, as all major tourist attractions are connected by public buses and the city's delightful **streetcars**. The latter are authentic reproductions (except for the rubber tires!) of San Antonio's rail streetcars from over fifty years ago. Passengers pay a nominal ten cent fare to be taken all around the downtown area. Guided tours are also readily available, both by bus or on foot. If you feel like exploring the city for yourself, pick up a do-it-yourself walking tour guide and don't hesitate to ask the friendly, hospitable locals for directions.

FIESTA SAN ANTONIO

San Antonio is world-renowned as a city of festivals ("fiestas"), and the most important is without a doubt "**la Fiesta San Antonio**" in mid-April, a special time due to the fine weather and flower blossoms. The "Fiesta" has been celebrated for over a hundred years, cancelled only during the two world wars. Its origins date back to 1891 when an élite group of wealthy women from San Antonio's Old South and German aristocratic families organized a small "**Battle of Flowers Parade**" with a Fiesta Queen and twelve flower-bedecked carriages from which women pelted spectators, and each other, with flowers to commemorate the Battles of the Alamo and San Jacinto. The festival grew over the years until the "Battle of the Flowers Parade," the largest parade in the U.S. organized and put on entirely by women, became only a part of the much larger "**Fiesta San Antonio**."

An élite men's association, the **Texas Cavaliers** was formed in 1926 to select a Fiesta King and assist the all-women's **Battle of Flowers Association** in the organization and management of the Fiesta. The **Texas Cavaliers' River Parade** was added at that time and the colorful procession of illuminated barges and boats along the San Antonio River quickly became an integral part of the festivities, drawing tens of thousands of spectators. But actual participation in the Fiesta was still fairly restricted to San Antonio's white social élite, with Hispanics, Blacks, and the lower classes present chiefly as spectators.

In 1947 the **League of United Latin American Citizens**, in order to ensure the participation in the Fiesta of the city's majority Hispanic population and lower classes, and so as to focus the city's attention on their problems, organized the election of the first "**El Rey Feo**" ("The Ugly King") to preside over a "**Fiesta Flambeau**" night-time parade with burning torches through the darkened streets of downtown. The spectacular procession, the largest of its kind in the world, has served greatly over the years to extend participation in Fiesta events to ever broader sectors of the population, and the money raised goes towards scholarships for Hispanic students.

In 1959 the **Fiesta San Antonio Commission** was formed to better organize and coordinate what was by then a vastly expanded Fiesta. Almost 100 non-profit organizations and over 50,000 volunteers work with the Commission throughout the year to organize the Fiesta which now lasts ten days. Besides the three major parades already mentioned, there are now more than 300 other events such as concerts, art shows, sporting events, festivals, elegant balls, and fireworks.

A Mexican "**charreada**," the rodeo originating with Mexican "rancheros" in the 1550s, is held at the beginning and end of the Fiesta. The Mexican American Chamber of Commerce sponsors a festival called "**La Noche de Fiesta**." And the enormous **Band Festival** is one of the biggest Fiesta events.

Adding to the carnival-like atmosphere are the "**cascarones**" which revelers smash over each other's heads throughout the festival: brightly-colored eggs carefully emptied of their contents through a small hole and then filled with confetti.

One of the most elaborate and popular events during the Fiesta is the **Night in Old San Antonio** (NIOSA), which originated in 1937 with a small Native American Festival at the San José Mission. Today NIOSA is a mega-production held in San Antonio's historic **La Villita** district with four unforgettable nights of ethnic food, dancing, and music from all over the world. Fifteen different food areas serve over 100,000 people a night with delectable and often exotic cooking from more than thirty different ethnic groups.

OTHER FESTIVALS

Other important events during the course of the year include the **Return of the Chili Queens** on Memorial Day weekend when stands serving chili con carne and other Mexican specialities are set up in San Antonio's plazas at night as in the days of old. The **Cine Festival** in February is North America's oldest and largest international Latino film festival, sponsored by the prestigious **Guadalupe Cultural Arts Center**. The **Tejano Conjunto Festival** in March celebrates this special mixture of Mexican and German music originating in South Texas. The **Cinco de Mayo** ("5th of May") festival held in **Market Square** celebrates Mexican resistance against an invasion by the French at the Battle of Puebla in 1862. The **Diez y Seis** festival (September 16th) is a fantastic week-long celebration of Mexican independence with pageants, dances, a street parade, and other forms of entertainment.

The **Martin Luther King Day March** on the state holiday in late January commemorates the life of the slain civil rights leader. In October there is a German **Oktoberfest** and a Greek festival called **Funstival**, and on **St. Patrick's Day** the San Antonio River is dyed green and renamed the River Shannon for a day. The **San Antonio Festival** in June is an international festival of music with symphony orchestras, ballet, opera, and jazz. The **Starving Artists Show** features nearly 1,000 artists exhibiting and selling their works along the **River Walk** and in **La Villita**. A portion of the proceeds go to feed the hungry.

For twelve days in February there is a stupendous **Livestock Show and Rodeo** put on by some 3,000 volunteers with daring cowboy competitions, livestock judging, carnival rides and fun, games of skill, fiddlers' contests, rattlesnake handlers, pig races, puppet shows, dances, and country western stars at the **Joe and Harry Freeman Coliseum**.

DAY-TRIPS

And if San Antonio's attractions and festivals aren't enough, it's possible to go on any number of splendid day-trips. The **Alamo Farms Winery and Vineyard**, about 25 miles southeast of the Alamo, offers tours with an underground wine cellar and grape vines dating back to the establishment of the city's first Spanish mission in 1716. For horse racing fans, the **Bandera Downs** race track is a 30-minute drive to the northwest in the heart of Texas Hill Country. The "**dude ranches**" in the countryside surrounding San Antonio offer Old West hospitality and Mexican "charreada" rodeos.

The **Natural Bridge Cavern** is a twenty-minute ride to the north with tours of intriguing cave formations dating from 140 million years ago. Nearby one can tour the historic German settlement of **New Braunfels** begun in 1845.

Fredericksburg and **Kerrville** are two other historic German towns just north of the city. And for a trip south of the border, there is great shopping at **Nuevo Laredo** across the border from Laredo 150 miles to the south.

SAN ANTONIO HISTORY

San Antonio began as a **Coahuiltecan village** in the 17th century at the headwaters of the San Antonio River where the Alamo and La Villita are located today. The village was called by the name the Native Americans had given to the twisting, winding river: "**Yanaguana**" or "drunken old man going home at night." The Coahuiltecans were hunting and gathering bands of extended families living in harmony with the natural world throughout South Texas and northeastern Mexico. Their population was eventually decimated by the diseases and repression brought by the Spanish in the 18th century.

The Spanish Franciscan Padre Massenett arrived at Yanaguana in 1691 and promptly renamed it **San Antonio**. In 1718 the Spanish Governor Alarcon and Franciscan Padre Olivares established a garrison and mission on the spot. The Spanish Viceroy wanted a half-way post between the struggling missions in East Texas and the Spanish Presidio of Northern Mexico in Saltillo.

Spanish colonial strategy was based on "**the cross and the sword**:" forced conversion of the indigenous population to Roman Catholicism and

The convent walls and garden at **Mission San José** — "the Queen of the Texas Missions."

*San Antonio's most popular attraction: the downtown **El Paseo del Rio** or **River Walk**.*

*Colorfully-costumed passengers on a boat in the **Fiesta San Antonio**'s **Texas Cavaliers' River Parade**.*

military defense of the "interests" of New Spain from Native American resistance, in particular from that of the Lipan Apaches and Comanches, and from encroachment by other European imperial powers, in particular the French.

In 1724 the **San Antonio Mission** was relocated to the present site of **the Alamo**. In its early years, Native Americans living at the mission included members of the Sanas, Scipxames, Tamiques, Tops, Yutas, Cocos, Jaranames, Pataguas, Payayas, Yierbipiames, Kiowas, and Lipan Apaches. But even at the mission's peak in the 1740s and 1750s, there were only about 300 Native Americans living there.

In 1731 fifteen families from the **Canary Islands** were sent by the Spanish King to settle what until then had been a military garrison and mission, and the first municipal government in Texas was organized. Also in 1731, three missions from East Texas, in difficulty because of Native American resistance and French hostility, were relocated south of the San Antonio Mission. They were **Mission Concepcion**, **San José**, **San Juan**, and **Espada**. By 1847 San Antonio was a village of about 1,000, including the Native Americans at the mission.

The Spanish missions flourished in the 1770s and 1780s, but with increased **Apache** and **Comanche** **resistance**, and secularization of the missions in the early 1790s, they entered an irreversible decline. After secularization in 1793, mission lands were redistributed to the Native Americans living there and the buildings slowly began to fall into ruins.

THE ALAMO AND TEXAN INDEPENDENCE

In the 1819 Adams-Onis (or "Florida") Treaty with Spain, U.S. President James Monroe gave up any claim to the area of Texas. During Mexico's war of independence from Spain, the San Antonio area was the site of major battles. In 1821, U.S. citizen Moses Austin received permission from Spanish authorities to bring 300 families from the U.S.A. into Texas. With **Mexican independence** that same year, after 300 years of Spanish colonialism, Texas became a Mexican province.

The new revolutionary Mexican government reconfirmed the grant that the Spanish had made to Austin, and when he died after the project had barely begun, it was his son Stephen who brought the settlers to Texas in 1822. The **U.S. settlers** swore their allegiance and became dutiful citizens of Mexico. Less

The fiery ingredients which go into Texas **chili con carne**.
Chili powder, made from ground red chili peppers and
spices, is said to have originated in San Antonio.

On the following pages:

The **San Antonio skyline** with the red-stone, green- roofed **Bexar
County Courthouse** in the center, to the east the **Tower Life
Building**, and the **Marriott Hotel** and **Convention Center** in the
upper right corner.

than ten years later there were more than 20,000
Anglo-American settlers living in Texas, mostly from
the Slave States of the South. Many had brought
slaves with them in serious violation of Mexican law.

Hostility towards the Mexican government increased
among the Anglo-Texan settlers, as did Mexican
worries that the province was becoming too pro-U.S.
In 1830 Mexico restricted further U.S. settlement in
Texas, and then in 1833 **General Santa Anna** took
power. That same year the U.S. settlers in Texas
revolted against Mexican rule. The cities of Gonzales
and Goliad were captured by the pro-U.S. forces, and
then in December 1835, after the defeat of Mexican
General Cos by Texan forces under the command of
Ben Milam, San Antonio was taken.

These actions were seen as high treason by Mexicans.
The Texan settlers had become Mexican citizens after
accepting land in return for allegiance and the oath of
loyalty. Events in Texas seemed to confirm the
tendency of the U.S. towards "manifest destiny"

expansionism at the expense of its neighbor south of
the border.
In February 1836 General Santa Anna marched on
San Antonio with an estimated 1,500 to 2,500 troops.
The pro-independence forces, an estimated 189 men
who were chiefly U.S. citizens, two-thirds of whom had
recently arrived in Texas, took refuge in **the Alamo**
and there began a 13-day seige. Very few had been
in Texas for more than six years. There was at least
one slave, a man named John who had been deserted
by his owner. There were also some women, children,
and servants. A power struggle for command took
place between William Travis of South Carolina and
James Bowie of Tennessee, but the latter being
seriously ill, Travis took command.
Santa Anna's men were tired and cold after their
forced march across the plains. They were armed
with obsolete English "escopetas" and many were
inexperienced recruits. The Anglo-Texans, many of
them sharpshooters, had greater expertise in
weaponry than the Mexican forces, as well as better
cannons and arms.

After a 13-day stand-off, the Mexican forces managed to breech the north wall of the fort at dawn on March 6, 1836. After ninety minutes of fierce hand-to-hand combat, the Mexican forces defeated the Alamo rebels. All the fort's defenders were killed, including Travis, Bowie, and Tennessee frontiersman David Crockett, who had just arrived in Texas. The women, children, and servants inside the fort were spared by the Mexican forces who counted almost 600 dead of their own. Mexican Lieutenant José Maria Torres had bravely fought his way to the Alamo's flagpole, torn down the Texas flag (that of a company of volunteers from New Orleans), and raised the Mexican flag before being killed with his hand still on the flagpole. Unknown to the combatants at the Alamo, 59 Texan delegates meeting at the little town of Washington-on-the-Brazos had declared Texas an independent republic on March 2, 1836. On March 27, several hundred Texan rebels were executed for high treason by Mexican soldiers after surrendering at Goliad. But the Alamo seige had slowed Santa Anna's advance and given General Sam Houston time to raise an army.

*This traditionally dressed Mexican woman gets in on the bronco riding at a colorful **Mexican "charreada" rodeo**.*

*A Native American dance ceremony during the **Texas Folklife Festival**, a 4-day celebration of some 30 cultures at the **Institute of Texas Cultures** in **HemisFair Park** in August.*

An aerial view of **the Alamo**'s walled-in compound in the heart of downtown San Antonio, with the **Long Barracks Museum** in the left-hand corner, and the **Museum/Souvenir Shop** to the left of the church.

The facade of **the Alamo**: the original part dates from 1744 and the keystone is dated 1758. The U.S. Army restored the structure in 1849, adding two upper windows and the gable top to the facade and a roof.

A close-up of the facade of **the Alamo**.

On April 21, 1836 some 800 Texan and U.S. volunteers under the command of General Sam Houston — with cries of "Remember the Alamo! Remember Goliad!" — defeated an estimated 1,500 Mexicans under the command of Santa Anna at **San Jacinto** after an 18-minute battle. Santa Anna was taken prisoner and to obtain his release he agreed to withdraw Mexican troops south of the Rio Grande and to recognize the independence of Texas.
After Santa Anna was freed, the Mexican government refused to accept the treaty but made no military attempt to take back the province.

The new **Republic of Texas**, under the Lone Star flag, legalized slavery and sought admission to the United States. Despite pressure from Sam Houston, who served two terms as president of the new republic, and from other Anglo-Texans, anti-slavery forces in the North opposed its admission to the Union. It wasn't until 1845 that Texas was admitted as the 28th state with a joint resolution of Congress which required only a simple majority and was thus able to overcome the opposition of anti-slavery forces. Mexico, needless to say, did not recognize the U.S. annexation of Texas.

THE MEXICAN-AMERICAN AND CIVIL WARS

In 1846 U.S. President James Polk took office with the intention of seizing all Mexican territory between Texas and the Pacific, including California. Polk provoked war with Mexico by sending General Zachary Taylor to occupy Mexico north of the Rio Grande in May 1846. When a shoot-out with Mexican troops occurred, Polk declared war and invaded Mexico. Many in the U.S. had opposed the war, including Representative Abraham Lincoln from Illinois who tried to force Polk to admit that the shooting had taken place on what was clearly Mexican territory.

*Left, **the Alamo** lit at night.*

*The Moorish-style decorative stonework around the carved wooden doors of **the Alamo**.*

The Mexicans fought bravely to defend their country, but the U.S. invasion forces, at a terrible price, eventually managed to defeat them. In February 1848 the **Treaty of Guadalupe Hidalgo** was signed in which Mexico gave up all claims to Texas as well as to what is today California, Nevada, and Utah, and parts of Arizona, Wyoming, Colorado and New Mexico. The U.S.A. had taken 1,200,000 square miles of territory from Mexico!
After the Mexican-American War, the years up until the Civil War saw a large influx of settlers into Texas, from the Southern Slave States and Germany in particular. In 1861 Texas seceded from the U.S. with the other Slave States of the **Confederacy**. With the victory of the Union forces in 1865, slavery was finally abolished throughout the United States, and Texas was readmitted to the Union in 1870 after ratifying the

15th Amendment to the Constitution, which stated that the right to vote could not be denied on the basis of "race, color, or previous condition of servitude."

In the late 1800s after the Civil War, San Antonio became an important center of the **cattle industry**. The Texas longhorn was developed by breeding English and Spanish cattle, and these cattle were driven north from the San Antonio Valley along the "long drive" to Kansas, where they were then sent on by rail to the Chicago slaughterhouses.
With the arrival of **railroads** and **military bases**, industry came to the San Antonio area. The discovery of **oil** near San Antonio at the beginning of the century further stimulated economic growth. And today San Antonio is the undisputed commercial and financial center of South Texas.

The Spanish Colonial-style facade of the modern **Museum/Souvenir Shop** at **the Alamo**, with the **Morgan Hotel** in the background.

A cool shaded fountain in **the Alamo** gardens.

A cannon seems to stand guard over the curving arches in the remaining walls of the **Long Barracks**, now a museum.

On the following pages:

The Alamo beautifully lit after another Texas sunset.

THE ALAMO TODAY

Established in 1718 as **Mission San Antonio de Valero**, the Alamo was relocated on its current site in 1724. With its secularization in 1793, the mission was closed and its lands were distributed to the resident Native Americans. In 1801 a Spanish cavalry unit from El Alamo de Parras was stationed at the former mission, and it is unclear whether the fort took its name from these soldiers or from the surrounding cottonwood trees ("alamo" is Spanish for cottonwood).

Today **the Alamo** and its walled-in, landscaped grounds are a green oasis in the heart of busy downtown San Antonio. All that remains of the original fort are the church and part of the walls of the convento (now the Long Barrack Museum walls). The church, in early baroque style with a decorative facade and massive wooden doors, was begun in 1744 , but never finished. It has no bell tower. Modern buildings near the chapel include the Long Barracks Museum, with relics dating from the Republic of Texas and audiovisual presentations on the Battle of the Alamo, the Museum/Souvenir shop, and the Daughters of the Texas Republic Library and meeting hall. Across from the Alamo is a white marble cenotaph done by the sculptor Coppini in 1936 to commemorate the defenders of the Alamo who fell in the 1836 battle.

Across the street from the Alamo are the **Plaza Theater of Wax** and **Ripley's Believe It or Not**. The wax museum displays some 200 figures from Hollywood, horror, and Texas history. Ripley's has eight major theme galleries with over 500 exhibits of

*Across from **the Alamo**, the gothic stonework of the **Emily Morgan Hotel**, the tallest building west of the Mississippi at the time of its construction in 1926, reflects the colors of the sunset.*

*The colonial-style **Menger Hotel** was built across Crockett Street from **the Alamo** in 1859 and came to be considered "the finest hotel between New Orleans and San Francisco."*

"the bizarre and the beautiful." The **Cowboy Museum and Gallery** is also in Alamo Plaza and includes a replica of a Western town and historical exhibits and artifacts showing how people in the Old West lived. There is also a Western art gallery and gift shop.

Two of San Antonio's finest old hotels are also across from the Alamo.

The **Emily Morgan Hotel** (705 E.Houston) is a historical landmark with a richly decorated gothic facade and windows and was the tallest building west of the Mississippi when built in 1926. Originally a medical building, it has been a hotel since 1983, taking its name from **Emily Morgan**, an ex-slave and mistress of Santa Anna who passed important military information on to the Texas independence forces.

The **Menger Hotel** with its colonial-style rooms was built on the Alamo Plaza by William Menger in 1859 and was soon considered "the finest hotel between New Orleans and San Francisco." The hotel's famous bar was built in 1887 and modelled after the one in the House of Lords in London.

Teddy Roosevelt recruited his "Rough Riders" there for combat in the conquest and occupation of Cuba during the 1898 Spanish-American War. The hotel served as their temporary home. It was completely restored in 1989, and there is an **Alamo Visitor Center** for information.

*Three spectacular night-time views of the gaily-lit bridges and trees of the **River Walk**, with its European-style sidewalk cafés.*

On the following pages:

*Enjoy great Tex-Mex cuisine at a riverside restaurant, where you can relax over a cold Corona or margarita as you people-watch on the **River Walk**.*

*A section of the **River Walk** with the **Hilton Palacio del Rio Hotel** in the background.*

THE RIVER WALK

After the Alamo, San Antonio is best known for its magnificent **Paseo del Rio** or "**River Walk**." Stretching about two and a half miles through the heart of downtown San Antonio from the **King William District** in the south to the **Municipal Auditorium** in the north, the River Walk dates from the years 1939-41. It is literally a paradise in the midst of San Antonio's busiest commercial district, winding along the jade-green San Antonio River twenty feet below street level for the equivalent of some 21 city blocks.

But if the River Walk exists today and continues to be extended, it is largely thanks to the **San Antonio Conservation Society** (SACS). The SACS was founded in 1925 and has played an important role in

the restoration and preservation of the city's architecture and natural environment ever since. In the 1920s, city businessmen proposed to cover what is today the River Walk, a horseshoe bend formed by a branch of the river downtown, with concrete and turn it into a sewer. The SACS waged a successful battle to preserve the area, and today the River Walk is San Antonio's most popular attraction.

Stone steps lead down to the River Walk from San Antonio's busy streets, and there is access for the physically handicapped at several points. Sections of the cobblestone walkways are tranquil and parklike with lush green subtropical foliage. Over 75 different types of trees shade the river's peaceful banks with tall cypresses older than the Alamo, as well as

*Elegant riverfront hotels open onto the lush tropical vegetation along the **River Walk**.*

*Over 75 different kinds of trees shade the **River Walk**'s luxuriant river banks.*

splendid oaks, willows, crepe myrtle, bananas, palms — all beautifully illuminated at night. Colorful gardens of bougainvillea and other flowering ornamental plants border the walkways.

Other sections of the River Walk are lined with European-style sidewalk cafés, multiethnic restaurants, fine shops, art galleries, night clubs, and hotels. Small waterfalls decorate the steps leading up to the Hyatt Hotel. The River Walk is unsurpassed for sightseeing, people-watching, or simply a peaceful stroll away from the hustle and bustle of downtown. River boats ferry passengers up and down the river on 40-minute excursions, while dining boats cruise along the river serving fine cuisine by candlelight. An unforgettable experience!

The River Walk is also a central location for many of San Antonio's yearly festivities. The **Holiday River Festival** in November-December begins with a sunset ceremony lighting 70,000 lights strung across the River Walk's bridges and trees and a parade of gaily decorated river boats accompanying the arrival of Santa Claus with his reindeer. At Christmas the River Walk is illuminated by the glow of thousands of candles in the **Fiesta de las Luminarias** ("Festival of Lights"), and Christmas carolers aboard river barges commemorate the Holy Family's search for lodging in the **Las Posadas** procession.

The River Walk is also central to **Fiesta San Antonio**. In fact the Fiesta King arrives on one of the decorated river barges in the **Texas Cavaliers' River Parade**. Other events on the River Walk during the course of the year include the **Fiesta Noche del Rio**, the **Starving Artist Show**, the **Great Country River Festival**, and the **Carnaval del Rio**.

*An aerial view of **La Villita** historical district with **La Villita Assembly Hall** on the left.*

__La Villita__ has many finely-restored historic buildings.

*Handwoven blankets and rugs for sale in **La Villita**.*

LA VILLITA

La Villita means "little town" and is on the site of what was once **Yuanaguana**: a walled village of the Coahuiltecan Native Americans on the east bank of the San Antonio River. Later when Canary Islanders arrived in 1731, it became San Antonio's first European settlement. Today it is a beautifully landscaped National Register Historic District occupying an entire city block between South Alamo and South Presa Streets, across from **HemisFair Plaza** and the **Convention Center**, and adjacent to the **River Walk** in the center of downtown San Antonio.

La Villita still resembles the original Spanish settlement of over 250 years ago. Stone walls surround the area's brick and tile paved streets and plazas. The entire area has been newly restored — thick-walled haciendas rise alongside adobe shops and galleries in Spanish Colonial-style patios and plazas, together with early Victorian and natural cut limestone buildings. All is beautifully planted with bananas, bougainvillea, and other flowering shrubs.

La Villita today is a center of arts, crafts, and entertainment with more than two dozen artisans' workshops and some very good restaurants. The atmosphere is that of a past era. Workshops practice glass-blowing, spinning and weaving, woodwork,

and jewelry and doll making. The shopping is great for handwoven blankets and rugs, Southwestern clothing and accessories, and terracotta. Be sure to take time out for a Bavarian or Mexican pastry.

La Villita also has a post office and many restored historical buildings. Of particular note is the **Cos House**, built in 1835 and then site of Mexican General Cos' surrender to the Anglo-Texans that same year. The **Old San Antonio Museum** has an interesting Texas History Collection, and you can get a cup of great coffee outdoors.

La Villita is also the site of many of San Antonio's yearly festivals including **Fiesta San Antonio's Night in Old San Antonio**: a multiethnic eating extravaganza attracting tens of thousands for four nights in April. Have a margarita at a sidewalk café with nacho chips and salsa or guacamole while deciding where to start. Tex-Mex? Try the mesquite-grilled or chicken-fried steak with an ice cold Corona. Or Texas barbecue: baby back ribs, brisket, pork, and chicken cooked very slowly over a low fire with an infinity of different barbecue sauces. Mexican? Pick from tacos, burritos, enchiladas, chiles rellenos, fajitas, tamales calientes, or simply have a "pan dulce" pastry. And that's just the local food!

ARNESON THEATRE

The **Arneson Theatre** is an outdoor theater in **La Villita** on the **River Walk**. The river divides the Spanish Mission-style stage from the sloping graded steps on the opposite bank, where the public can enjoy mariachis, flamenco, opera, jazz, and country western performances. The theater is also the site for the **Fiesta Noche del Rio** in the summer and part of the **Great Country River Festival** with three days of free country western music in September.

HERTZBERG CIRCUS COLLECTION

Near the **Arneson Theatre** is the **Hertzberg Circus Collection** with over 20,000 items from the circus world. The historical development of the circus is traced from its English origins to P.T. Barnum and the three-ring circus in the U.S. Curiosities include an antique circus poster collection, Tom Thumb's carriage, and a scale model of a three-ring circus.

*Two views of the **Arneson River Theatre**, where a branch of the San Antonio River separates the Spanish Colonial-style stage from the audience, seated on the graded steps of the amphitheater on the opposite bank.*

*The striking costumes of the dancers in a flamenco performance at the **Arneson River Theatre**.*

*The 3-story glass facade of the **Rivercenter Mall** on a branch of the river downtown, and a detail of the carved stonework on the street-side facade.*

*The stately stone facade and tower of **St.Joseph's Church** downtown on Commerce Street.*

RIVERCENTER

Around the corner from **the Alamo** and across a branch of the river from the **Convention Center** is the **Rivercenter Mall**, a 3-level glass complex with 135 shops and restaurants, a 1,000-room hotel opened in 1988, and a new office tower. The mall is also home to the **Imax Theatre** which shows a 45-minute documentary on the Battle of the Alamo. The screen is six stories high — ten times bigger than a normal movie screen — and has six-track stereo sound, all of which gives the audience a real sense of participation in the action.

MUNICIPAL AUDITORIUM

The **San Antonio Municipal Auditorium** was built in Mediterranean style in 1926. It was restored after a 1975 fire, reopening in 1985 after a $13 million renovation. The main auditorium seats 5,000 people and is used for city events, meetings, and conventions. There are also smaller theaters on the premises.

SOUTHWEST CRAFT CENTER

A couple of blocks down river from the **Municipal Auditorium** on the opposite bank is the **Southwest Craft Center**. The Center is housed in the restored buildings and courtyard of the old **Ursuline Academy and Convent**, dating from 1848 — San Antonio's finest example of country French architecture. It is a community of skilled artisans creating, exhibiting, and selling their craftwork as well as offering arts and crafts classes. There is also dining at the Copper Kitchen restaurant.

MUNICIPAL AUDITORIUM

The magnificent Mediterranean-style facade of the **Municipal Auditorium**.

The splendid facade of the **Texas Theatre** on Houston Street is all that remains of the original structure.

The Alamodome with San Antonio's skyline in the distance. From left to right: the **Tower Life Building**, the **Tower of the Americas**, the **Convention Center Arena**, and the **Marriott Hotel**.

The **Henry B. Gonzalez Convention Center**: built for the 1968 **HemisFair** world's fair, and doubled in size when renovated in 1986.

ALAMODOME

Alamodome, San Antonio's impressive multipurpose indoor stadium which opened in 1993, has 65,000 seats with unobstructed view, and up to 72,000 spectators can be accommodated for football games. There are 160,000 square feet of floor space, and excellent facilities are provided for conventions, expositions, trade shows, and entertainment, as well as for major sports events including professional football with Houston Oilers' games, NBA basketball games with the San Antonio Spurs, and soccer. A permanent ice floor is used for skating events. The roof of the dome is suspended from cables anchored to four concrete towers, in the latest of state-of-the-art architecture. And conveniently, the Alamodome is only a few minutes walk from the **Convention Center** and the **River Walk** downtown.

HENRY B. GONZALEZ CONVENTION CENTER

San Antonio's **Convention Center** was originally constructed for **HemisFair** — the year-long world's fair held in San Antonio in 1968. Expansion and renovation were completed in 1986, and the Center was doubled in size to 516,506 square feet. It is located between East Market Street and **HemisFair Park** and, among other facilities, offers an Arena with more than 15,000 seats and a Theatre with more than 2,500. A mural by artist Juan O'Gorman "The Confluence of Civilizations in the Americas" adorns one of the Center's external walls.

The **Tower of the Americas** with the new **Alamodome** behind it on the right, and the **U.S.Court House** and **Federal Building** in the foreground.

The 750-foot **Tower of the Americas** at sunset.

On the following pages:

The city's first real skyscraper: the **Tower Life Building** in the heart of downtown San Antonio.

The colorfully-illuminated **Tower Life Building** after sunset.

HEMISFAIR PARK AND THE TOWER OF THE AMERICAS

HemisFair, the 1968 world's fair in San Antonio, provided the greatest impetus to the city's growth this century, helping to turn the city into the major tourist attraction it is today.

The year-long fair led to the restoration of the historic **La Villita** quarter and the renovation of the elegant 19th century houses in the residential **King William District**. Many spectacular modern buildings with galleries, hotels, restaurants, and shops were constructed, and the city inherited its **Convention Center**, a **Theater for the Performing Arts**, the **Institute of Texan Cultures**, as well as the **Tower of the Americas** and the constructions of **HemisFair Park** adjacent to the central business district.

The **Tower of the Americas** was constructed as a symbol of the confluence of civilizations in the Americas. The tower's antenna stretches 750 feet above the city, and glass-walled external elevators take visitors up to the almost 500-foot observation level and revolving restaurant. The panorama of the city and its surrounding countryside, with the hill country to the northwest and the plains stretching south, is breathtaking.

The **HemisFair Plaza Water Park**, constructed around the base of the tower in 1988, is beautifully landscaped with gardens and walkways, and a million gallons of water flow through the park's fountains, waterfalls, streams and ponds. Nearby is the **Downtown All-Around Playground** for kids.

The **Institute of Texan Cultures** was created as the Texas Pavilion for Hemis Fair in 1968 and is now a part of the University of Texas at San Antonio. The museum focuses on the contributions of 26 different ethnic groups to Texas history and folk culture. There are hands-on exhibitions and a collection of almost 800,000 photos dating from the late 1800s. The Dome Show is a multimedia exhibit with 36 screens showing the different "places and faces" of Texas. In addition there are numerous special events throughout the year.

Of particular note is the **Texas Folklife Festival** in August — a 4-day multiethnic celebration with entertainment, food, dance, arts and crafts, and games.

The **Instituto Cultural Mexicano**, the only institute of its kind outside of Mexico, was established in HemisFair Park in 1972 to promote San Antonio's Mexican heritage. Contemporary work by Mexican and other Latin American artists is exhibited, and there are lectures, films, and a gift shop with posters, artbooks, and Mexican folkart.

A couple of blocks due east of HemisFair Park on East Houston Street is the **Carver Community Cultural Center**, exhibiting the art and culture of Black America.

37

*The twin-towered Spanish Colonial facade of the **San Fernando Cathedral**, built by settlers from the Canary Islands in the 1730s.*

*San Antonio's most important theater: the **Majestic Performing Arts Center**, beautifully restored to its original 1929 appearance.*

*The theater's interior at the **Majestic Performing Arts Center** is elaborately decorated in Spanish Colonial and Moorish style.*

SAN FERNANDO CATHEDRAL

San Antonio's twin-towered, gold-domed **San Fernando Cathedral** was built by settlers from the Canary Islands in 1734 and is the oldest cathedral sanctuary in the U.S., and the oldest parish church in Texas. Mexican General Santa Anna raised the flag of "Deguello" ("no quarter") from one of the cathedral's towers during the Battle of the Alamo in 1836, thereby advising the fort's 188 defenders, who had refused to surrender during the 13-day siege, that it would be a fight to the death.

Down the street from the cathedral is San Antonio's historic romanesque-style **Bexar County Courthouse**, built in 1895 of red Texas granite and sandstone. Adjacent to the courthouse is the recently finished **Bexar County Justice Center** with 16 modern courtrooms and a 600-car parking garage. San Antonio's **City Hall** is behind the cathedral.

SPANISH GOVERNOR'S PALACE

Facing City Hall is the **Spanish Governor's Palace** — called "the most beautiful building in San Antonio" by the National Geographic Society. Built in 1722, this National Historic Landmark is the only remaining Spanish Colonial residence in Texas and once housed officials of the Spanish Province of Texas. Over the entrance a carved keystone, with the Hapsburg coat-of-arms, indicates that construction was finished in 1749. The palace has a large cobblestone patio with a fountain and lush garden, walls which are almost three feet thick, stone floors, and original Spanish-period furnishings. Down the street is the **José Navarro House** — the restored home and office of the only native Texan to participate in the convention ratifying the annexation of Texas by the U.S. It is a State Historic Site.

MARKET SQUARE

Across the street from the **Spanish Governor's Palace** is San Antonio's fabulous **Market Square**, dating from the mid-1800s. Its plazas, lit by Victorian street lamps, are lined with interesting shops and restaurants and are alive with activity, including Mariachi music and Mexican dances, from the early morning until late into the night. The square is the location for many of San Antonio's yearly festivals, including **Cinco de Mayo** and the **Return of the Chili Queens** in May, and the Mexican Christmas festival **Las Fiestas Navideñas** with piñata parties, the blessing of the animals, and a visit from "Pancho Claus." At the **Farmers' Market**, fresh produce can be bought in the early morning directly from the farmer. The **Centro de Artes del Mercado** ("Market Square Cultural Center") is in a renovated 2-story building from 1922 and holds exhibitions, conferences, and concerts. **El Mercado** is a large indoor shopping area with old but renovated Spanish constructions across from **Milam Park**, modelled after a typical Mexican market. Over 35 Mexican specialty shops offer unique handcrafted goods in an authentic Mexican market atmosphere, and fine restaurants serve excellent Mexican food outdoors under large umbrellas.

*The peaceful **King William** section of the **River Walk**, with the **Tower Life Building** rising up in the distance.*

*A 1983 reproduction of the **Johnson Street Foot Bridge**, built at Commerce Street in 1880, moved to the present site in 1914, and removed in 1960. It is also called the O. Henry Bridge, after the author who used it in some of his short stories.*

MAJESTIC PERFORMING ARTS CENTER

The **Majestic Theatre** is the most important of San Antonio's over a dozen theaters and home to the **San Antonio Symphony**. In 1981 the theater, rich in architectural ornamentation, was restored to its original 1929 appearance — one of the few remaining vintage vaudeville/movie theaters. It hosts all sorts of performances, from touring Broadway shows to national theatrical productions and rock concerts with big-name artists.

KING WILLIAM DISTRICT

The stately **King William Quarter** is a 25-block historic district, the city's first, not far from downtown on the south bank of the river. The area was originally settled by prominent German merchants and was San Antonio's most elegant residential district during the late 1800s. It was renovated in 1968, at the time of HemisFair, and is once again fashionable, with beautifully restored Victorian and early Texas houses. The King William Association or the San Antonio Conservation Society can provide information and maps for walking tours of the district.

The **Steves Homestead** (509 King William St.), now a museum, was a fashionable 3-story German residence built around 1876 in Victorian French Second Empire style. Made of smooth-dressed ashlar limestone, the house is one of the finest examples of the Victorian style in the Southwest.

The **Carl H. Guenther House** (129 E. Guenther) is now a historical museum, with a fine collection of Dresden plates and material concerning the development of the Pioneer Flour Mills company — a river mill which was established on the site in 1859. Today it is the oldest continuously operating flour mill in Texas. The house also contains a shop and restaurant.

Another attraction is the **Buckhorn Hall of Horns, Fins, and Feathers** with over 3,500 animal trophies and the **Buckhorn Saloon**, an authentic unaltered Old West saloon, both on the grounds of the Lone Star Brewery (600 Lone Star Boulevard).

The **Steves Homestead**, built around 1876, is one of the finest examples of Victorian architecture in the Southwest.

The **Carl H. Guenther House** is today a museum on the spot where the **Pioneer Flour Mills** company was established in 1859.

The **Anton Wulff House** with the Tower Life Building in the distance. The house was built of local limestone in about 1870 and is today the home of the **San Antonio Conservation Society**.

The **George Kalteyer House**, built in 1892, was designed by the same Texas architect who did the **Bexar County Courthouse** in San Antonio.

*The symmetrical bell towers of the **Mission Concepción**'s limestone church, constructed so well that it has never been restored since completion in 1755.*

*The roofed arcade of the convento, with arches opening onto the patio and well, at **Mission Concepción**.*

THE SPANISH MISSIONS

The Spanish established almost forty Catholic missions in Texas, the greatest concentration in North America, and five of them were located along the river in San Antonio due to the relatively large population of **Coahuiltecans** in the area. The Spanish colonial strategy of establishing military garrisons ("presidios") and missions together — "the cross and the sword" — had already worked to expand the empire in Mexico and Peru and was now being employed across the North American Southwest.

The missions' aggressive program of coercive conversion to Roman Catholicism was an integral part of Spanish colonialist expansion. Native Americans living in the missions were submitted to a very rigid and authoritarian social, moral, and religious discipline. Work was long and hard. Many Native Americans rejected the white man's faith and were hostile to mission life, and the missionaries attempted to recapture those who ran away. They were often conscripted by the military when it was

necessary to defend Spanish interests from other hostile Native Americans or other colonial powers. There were never more than a few hundred living on the San Antonio missions, even when they were at their peak in the years between 1745 and 1775.

By the late 18th century, the missions were in irreversible decline as a result of heightened resistance to the Spanish presence by Native American forces, Apaches and Comanches in particular, and as a result of the decimation of the local native populations caused by European-brought diseases. All Texas missions were secularized by the revolutionary Mexican government in 1824, and their lands were distributed to the Native Americans living there. Most of their buildings gradually turned to ruins as the years passed.

The missions were constructed in a variety of architectural styles brought over from Spain, including Moorish, Renaissance, Romanesque and

Gothic, by skilled craftsmen from Mexico with Native American labor. Most missions had a church, a granary, Native American quarters, a tannery, a blacksmith, and textile shops, all as part of a defensive wall around a large inner courtyard defended with bastions and cannons. The farm lands were outside the mission walls, and most missions had a ranch a few miles away. The missions served the Spanish empire as churches, fortresses, Native American pueblos, soldiers' barracks, schools, and granaries.

San Antonio de Valero, better known as **the Alamo**, was the first mission in the San Antonio area, established in 1718 and relocated to its present site in 1724. The other four missions were relocated along the San Antonio River south of the Alamo from East Texas in 1731. Today they are still active parish churches, among the country's oldest, and together comprise the **San Antonio Missions National Historic Park** which stretches along the **Mission Trail** following the winding river south for nine miles. San Antonio is one of the few U.S. cities to have a National Historic Park within its city limits. Each of the four missions has been assigned a different "theme" by the park service.

To visit the missions along Mission Trail, take the city bus or drive. Picnic and camping facilities are available near the missions, but beware of the fire ants when straying from the sidewalk!

MISSION CONCEPCIÓN

Mission Nuestra Senora de la Purisima Concepción de Acuna, the first along the **Mission trail**, is the oldest unrestored Texas mission and Catholic Church in the U.S. Originally established in 1716 in East Texas among the **Tejas Native Americans** who gave their name to the state, it was relocated to its present site in 1731. The church, made of tufa limestone, was finished in 1755 and has symmetrical twin towers and a Moorish cupola. The facade is decorated with sculptured stonework framing large wooden doors. The walls are four feet thick and the floor is flagstone. The interior walls have some rare 18th century religious and decorative frescoes done by the missionaries and Native Americans in red, blue, and ochre. The sacristy and several convent rooms still exist. Its interpretative theme is "the Mission as a Religious Center." Nearby is the restored adobe **Yturri-Edmunds Home and Mill** dating from the mid-1800s.

*The decorative carved stonework from the facade of the **Mission San José** church, including the famous "**Rosa's Window**.*

*A view of the Moorish-style dome, square bell tower, sacristy, arched convento wall, and stone well, seen from within the walls at **Mission San José**.*

MISSION SAN JOSE'

Mission San José y San Miguel de Aguayo, called "the Queen of the Missions," was the largest, most beautiful and prosperous, and best fortified of all Texas' missions.

Established in East Texas in 1720, it was relocated twice, finally arriving at its present site in 1731.

Today the mission is surrounded by about seven acres of rural countryside,
and most of the original mission square has been preserved.

Construction on the tufa limestone church began in 1768 and was finished in 1782. Its exceptional facade is adorned with ornate baroque sculptured stonework and massive carved doors, and there is a square bell tower, a well-preserved sacristy, and a stone-carved window, "Rosa's Window," which is considered one of the finest examples of Spanish Colonial decorative work in the U.S.

Within the walls of the Mission there are: five cloisters; a Native American pueblo with 84 compartments; a 5,000-bushel capacity granary with massive flying buttresses, from about 1749, and perhaps the oldest standing stone building in Texas; and a "baluarte" or fortified corner tower with 3-foot thick walls, and holes for cannons and rifles which allowed defenders to protect two of the mission's external walls during the frequent Apache and Comanche attacks.

Outside the north wall is a restored mill, built around 1789-1794, with a horizontal water wheel.

The mission's interpretive theme is: "the Mission as a Social Center and as a Center of Defense."

*The austere architecture of **Mission San Juan** seen from within the mission walls.*

*The church facade at **Mission Espada**, with carved wooden doors in an arched stone doorway which is strangely inverted. The facade is crowned by an open bell tower like at **San Juan**, with three bells and a small iron cross at its summit. In the foreground is the stone well of the convento.*

MISSION SAN JUAN

Mission San Juan Capistrano was originally established in 1716 in East Texas among the Nazoni Native Americans. Its simple, stark architectural style is not as striking as that of the other missions. The chapel has an open bell tower with three bells and a small iron cross at its summit. There are cornstock pith figures of Jesus and Mary made with a process developed by the Native Americans of Central Mexico and lost soon after the Spanish conquest.

Most of the original walled-in mission square remains and gives a good idea of a typical mission layout: church, convento (now a historical museum), Native American quarters, and the ruins of the "hospederia" (guest lodgings). The mission's theme is "the Mission as an Economic Center."

MISSION ESPADA

Mission San Francisco de la Espada is the furthest from town and was thus the most exposed to Native American attacks. It was originally the first mission established in East Texas in 1690, and relocated to its present site in 1731. By 1778 the original mission structures were in ruins. Today only the chapel and information center are open to the public. The church has a red tile floor and a simple altar. Its facade is starkly simple except for the inverted Moorish-style arched stone doorway around the carved wooden doors. The mystery of the inverted doorway has never been solved: was it a mistake or intentional?

The open bell tower is similar to the one at **San Juan**, with three bells and a small iron cross at its summit. The mission walls contain an intact corner "baluarte" similar to the fortified tower at **San José**. The mission's interpretive theme is: "the Mission as a Vocational Education Center."

About a mile and a half north of the mission the **Espada Aqueduct** lifts water from the San Antonio River over Piedras Creek.
This National Historic Landmark was built by the mission's priests between 1731 and 1740. The priests also built a 270-foot dam and canal system. The dam still stands
and has held up against all floods for the last two centuries. The mission's still-functioning irrigation system was based on the system which the Moslems had introduced in Spain.

MUSEUM OF ART

North of downtown but before **Brackenridge Park** is the **San Antonio Museum of Art** located at 200 West Jones Avenue in the old Lone Star Brewery building. Listed in the National Register of Historic Places, the renovated turn-of-the-century brewery complex, with glass elevators, skylights, and a skywalk, is a delight in itself. The Museum's collection ranges from antiquity to contemporary art, and includes archaeological relics, Greek and Roman sculpture, and a pre-Columbian gallery of Central American and Peruvian ceramics, sculpture and pottery from the Colima, Nayarit, Jalisco, Olmec, and Mayan cultures. There are also Spanish Colonial objects, Asian art and Chinese porcelains, Mexican folk art, and 17th-19th century European and 18th-19th century American art. The Museum also hosts frequent traveling exhibits.

McNAY MUSEUM

The **Marion Koogler McNay Museum** is north of **Brackenridge Park** at 6000 North New Braunsfels Avenue. The Museum is housed in its namesake's former Andalusian-Mediterranean style mansion, designed by San Antonio architects Robert and Atlee B. Ayres. The grounds are lovely, and the patio and gardens are a favorite spot for wedding photos. The museum has works by painters, graphic artists, and sculptors from the 19th and 20th centuries, in addition to Gothic and Medieval art, and early New

*The **San Antonio Museum of Art** in the reconverted old L one Star Brewery complex at 200 West Jones Avenue.*

*The **McNay Museum**'s art collection is housed in a Mediterranean-style mansion on the park-like former estate of Marion Koogler McNay.*

Mexican arts and crafts. Its collection of Post-Impressionist painting is one of the finest in the U.S. Works are on exhibition by such artists as Cézanne, Gauguin, Picasso, Van Gogh, Monet, Matisse, Goya, Renoir, Rauschenberg, and de Kooning, among others.

Next door to the **McNay Museum** is the **San Antonio Art Institute** — a new art college with library, auditorium, offices, classrooms, and gallery space exhibiting contemporary painting, printmaking, sculpture, and design by emerging young artists from around Texas and the rest of the country.

WITTE MUSEUM

The **Witte Museum**, a city landmark since its foundation in 1926, is a regional museum with hands-on, changing exhibits on natural science, anthropology, and Native American and Texas history. Permanent exhibitions include: "Texas Wild: Ecology Illustrated" with walk-through dioramas of South Texas Brushland and the state's six other natural regions; and "Ancient Texans: Rock Art and Lifeways along the Lower Pecos," the culture and rock paintings of a hunter-gatherer society in southwest Texas 8,000 years ago. Other attractions include an exhibition of dinosaurs from 65 million years ago, an "EcoLab" with live Texas animals, an outdoor "Butterfly and Hummingbird Garden," and three restored historic homes.

*The **Witte Museum** in 433-acre **Brackenridge Park**: a city landmark since 1926.*

SAN ANTONIO ZOO

The **San Antonio Zoological Gardens and Aquarium**," just west of the **Witte Museum** in **Brackenridge Park**, is the 3rd largest animal collection in North America, with over 3,500 specimens of 800 different species, from the snow leopard to the polar bear, and it's one of the finest zoos in the world. It spreads over more than fifty acres at the headwaters of the San Antonio River in an old rock quarry with limestone cliffs and lots of oak, pecan, and cypress trees. With its rocky outcroppings, the quarry facilitates the re-creation of a natural environment for the animals, with barless cages and open pits and ditches. Animals live together in family groupings wherever possible.

There is also a "zoo nursery" for baby animals; in fact the zoo has an international reputation for breeding in captivity, which includes the first white rhino born in the U.S. The zoo's collection of African antelopes is one of the largest and most varied in the world, and there are a "monkey island" and a "hippo pond" as well. There is also an oustanding bird collection including penguins, flamingos, and other exotic species, and it's the only zoo in the world to exhibit a whooping crane. In addition, the zoo offers elephant rides and, at the children's zoo, boat rides.

A koala bear, military macaws, and a baby tiger at the **San Antonio Zoo***.*

*The young Japanese couple that once ran the **Japanese Tea Garden** was forced out by the racist hysteria accompanying World War II, and the name was changed to the "Chinese Tea Garden." The city recently changed the name back to the original.*

*Looking down on the **Japanese Tea Garden**'s sunken gardens and goldfish ponds.*

*A view of the 38-acre gardens at the San Antonio **Botanical Center**.*

JAPANESE TEA GARDEN

The exquisite **Japanese Tea Garden** at the northwest edge of **Brackenridge Park** is always open and there is no admission charge. A young Japanese family ran a tea room on the site of these sunken gardens before World War II, but with the anti-Japanese racist hysteria which accompanied the outbreak of the war in the Pacific, they were forced out, and the name was changed to "Chinese Tea Garden." Recently the city changed its name back to the original in a ceremony with descendents of the original Japanese family.

The sunken gardens include a great variety of plants and floral displays, with winding pebble paths and stone bridges over irregularly-shaped ponds filled with water lilies and goldfish, and there is a 60-foot waterfall. The gardens are set in an old limestone quarry which had been used to provide the stone to construct the state capitol in Austin as well as many San Antonio homes.

BOTANICAL CENTER AND HALSELL CONSERVATORY

A couple of blocks east of **Brackenridge Park**, on the opposite side from the **Japanese Tea Room**, is the **San Antonio Botanical Center** and the **Lucile Halsell Conservatory** at 555 Funston Place. The Botanical Center is a 38-acre garden recreating three different regional landscapes: the East Texas piney woods, the Southwest Texas plains, and the Central Texas hill country. There is a fragrance and touch garden for the visually handicapped.

The **Conservatory** is a $6.5 million, 90,000-square-foot complex of climatically-controlled underground greenhouses. Among the top ten botanical centers in the country, its architecture is incredible. A 16-foot tunnel leads below ground to a large inner courtyard and pond. Around the courtyard are an exhibition hall, tropical house, desert house, palm house, fern room, and orangerie. Amazing!

The landmark **Taj Mahal** water tower at **Randolph Air Force Base**.

The **Missing Man Monument** at **Randolph Air Force Base**.

The war memorial at the **U.S. Army Medical Museum** at **Fort Sam Houston**.

Vietnam Veterans Memorial.

MILITARY BASES

The Spanish founded San Antonio as a military garrison in 1718, and it has been the site of military bases ever since. Today there are one army and four air force bases. A visitor's pass is normally required except at the **Fort Sam Houston** army base which is an open post.

Fort Sam Houston was established in 1876 and is a historic landmark. It was originally the southern-most of a string of U.S. forts guarding westward routes to California. The 500-acre fort is one of the oldest U.S. military posts still in use, and presents a park-like setting with animals and birds around an old quadrangle dating back to 1876. Here Native American guerrilla leader Geronimo and his Apache chiefs were imprisoned, and troops were raised to pursue the Mexican revolutionary leader Pancho Villa into Mexico. The fort is also home to the **Brooke Army Medical Center**, one of the largest in the world, and the **U.S. Army Medical Museum**.

The four air force bases are **Brooks**, **Kelly**, **Randolph**, and **Lackland Air Force Bases**. **Brooks** is home to the "School of Aerospace Medicine." **Randolph** is headquarters for the "Air Training Command" and is the "U.S. Air Force Military Personnel Center." The base is known for its landmark **Taj Mahal** water tower. **Kelly** is home to the "Air Logistics Center." Adjacent to Kelly is **Lackland**, the largest military training center in the U.S. Every air force recruit goes through Lackland for basic training.

Shamu the killer whale performs in 4,500-seat Shamu Stadium.

State flags flap in the breeze at Sea World.

Feeding and petting Atlantic bottlenose dolphins at the Marine Mammal Pool.

SEA WORLD

Not far west of **Lackland Air Force Base** is **Sea World** — the largest marine life park and the largest marine mammal habitat in the world. Sea World opened in 1988, and it is now the biggest entertainment center in the whole Southwest. Sea World's 250 acres are only a 10-minute drive from downtown, and there are always dozens of shows, educational exhibits, and attractions at any one time. An in-park trolley car makes it easy to get around.

Killer whales "Shamu" and "Baby Shamu," performing in "The Legend of Shamu," "a spectacle of power, mystery, and Indian lore" in 4,500-seat Shamu Stadium, provide a truly unforgettable experience, and it's often a bit wet for those seated in the front rows! Baby Shamu is the first killer whale to be born and raised in captivity. Walruses, sea lions, and an otter give comic performances in "the Spooky, Kooky Castle Show" in a 3,000-seat stadium.

You can feed and touch (or shake fins with) the bottlenose dolphins at the "Marine Mammal Pool," and seals and sea lions at their "Seal and Sea Lion Community." The "Wet, Wild, and Wonderful" whale and dolphin show is superb. The world's largest collection of beluga whales really captures the imagination, and the otters' playful antics never stop. An Antarctic environment provides a home to more than 300 penguins — the largest home to penguins

outside of the Antarctic.

Sea World also has the largest collection of exotic Indo-Pacific fish in the world. There are a 300,000-gallon Coral Reef environment with tropical fish and a 450,000-gallon shark habitat. The only hammerhead sharks on display in North America are at Sea World. The colorful birds of the "Tropical Aviary" are magnificent, as are the flamingo and waterfowl exhibits. And there is an "Alligator Habitat" for reptile enthusiasts.

Other attractions include the acrobatic "All-Star Ski Revue" with expert world class water skiers, a new ice skating show, and "Lost Lagoon," a 5-acre water adventure area with water slides, an enormous wave pool, and sandy beach. Children can also play on the three acres of tropical fun at "Shamu's Happy Harbor" or at the "Cap'n Kid's World" play area. Plunging down 5-stories on the "Texas Splashdown" and riding the 1,800-foot-long "Rio Loco" rapids are two wild and wet water adventure rides.

The 16-acre "**Cypress Gardens West**" botanical garden offers a pleasant stroll along garden paths through flowers and moss-covered oak trees. And "Summer Night Magic" is a summer-long concert series with street entertainers and big-name artists and choreographed musical shows, brilliant fireworks displays, and flashing laser shows.

FIESTA TEXAS

Fiesta Texas is a newly opened (1992) 200-acre entertainment park set in an old limestone quarry with 100-foot cliffs northwest of the city. It is a musical celebration of Texas' different heritages, with shows, over a dozen amusement rides, restaurants and shops, and a schedule full of celebrations and festivals. Up to sixty live performances a day take place on seven stages located around the park. There are four major theme areas and the refreshing "Splashwater Springs" water park.

Visit the authentic little Mexican town of "**Los Festivales**," and take part in the festivities celebrating "El Dia de los Fundadores" (Founders' Day). Mexican singers and dancers enliven the streets and the Mexican street mercado, where you can pick up traditional gifts and craftwork as well as excellent Mexican food. Musical productions are performed in the "Zaragoza" or "Teatro Fiesta" theaters. Viva Mexico!

Celebrate "**Oktoberfest**" at the little Bavarian-style Texas village of "Spassburg," similar to those in the Texas Hill Country settled by German immigrants in the mid-1800s. The "Sangerfest Halle" offers great German music, food, and drink, and there are German crafts and great amusement rides for both adults and kids.

"**Crackaxle Canyon**" recreates life in the Southwest in the 1920s, with a Texas boom town celebration and "Old Blue's Texas Barbecue." Musical productions are put on at "Lone Star Lil's" and the "Sundance" theaters. "The Rattler" is the world's highest and fastest wooden roller coaster, and "the Gully Rusher" is a river rapids water ride.

And finally, the world of 1950s rock 'n' roll is recreated at a high school homecoming celebration in the small Texas town of "**Rockville**." Watch the homecoming parade with class floats, the school band, and of course the Queen and her court. The "Rockville Gym" hosts a musical show, and there are rock 'n' roll stars at the "Loop Drive-In." Rides include the "Power Surge," "Motorama," and the "Hustler." There is no better way to end a delightful day in San Antonio than with the fun and festivities at **Fiesta Texas**!

The world's fastest, tallest, and steepest wooden roller coaster, the **Rattler**, at **Fiesta Texas**.

The finale of **"Heart of Texas"** at the **Zaragoza Theater** in the Mexican town of "**Los Festivales**" at **Fiesta Texas**.

Sangerfest Halle in the German village of "**Spassburg**" at **Fiesta Texas**.

The **Lone Star Spectacular** ends each day at **Fiesta Texas** with fireworks and laser shows.

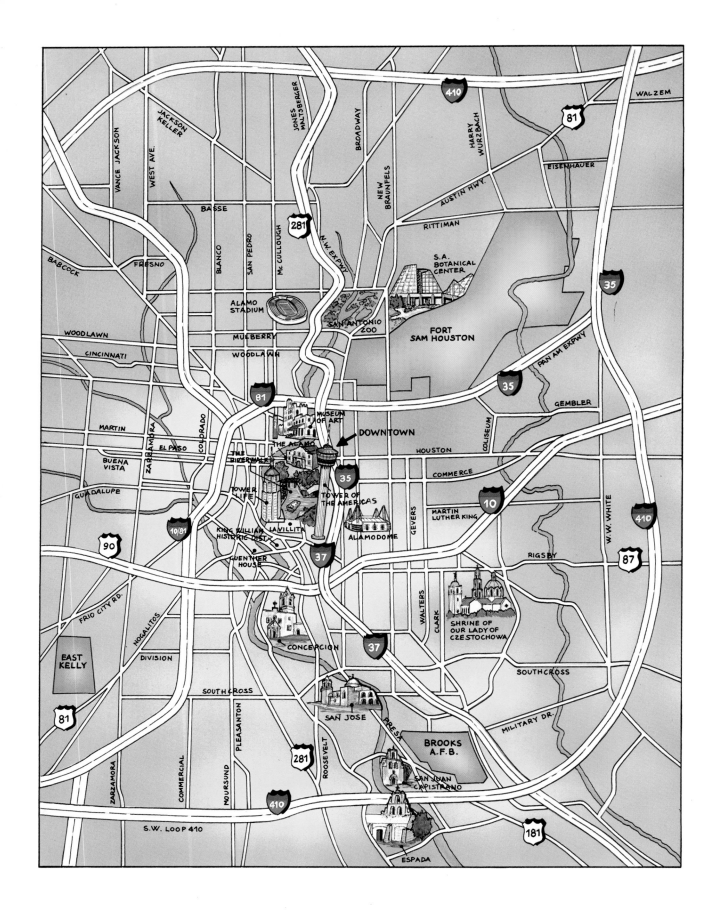